I Can Trick a Tiger

Written by Cynthia Rider

Illustrated by Alex Brychta

OXFORD
UNIVERSITY PRESS

Floppy was dreaming that
he was in the jungle.

A tiger jumped out.
"Got you!" he said.

"I can trick a tiger,"
said Floppy.

"Look out!" said Floppy.
"There's a bee on your nose."

"Oh no!" said the tiger,
and he let Floppy go.

A crocodile jumped out.
"Got you!" she said.

"I can trick a crocodile,"
said Floppy.

"Look out!" said Floppy.

"There's a bee on your nose."

"Oh no!" said the crocodile,
and she let Floppy go.

A snake slid out.

"Got you!" she said.

"I can trick a snake,"
said Floppy.

"Look out!" said Floppy.
"There's a bee on your nose."

"Oh no!" said the snake,
and she let Floppy go.

A rabbit jumped out.

"Got you!" said Floppy.

"Look out!" said the rabbit.

"There's a bee on your nose."

Buzzzzzzzzz!

"Oh no!" said Floppy.

Why did the tiger let Floppy go?

What would you do if you had a bee on your nose?

How do you think Floppy felt when the bee landed on his nose?

Have you ever played a trick on anybody?

Was it a funny trick?

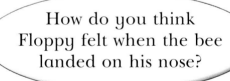

Rhyming words

Match the things that rhyme.

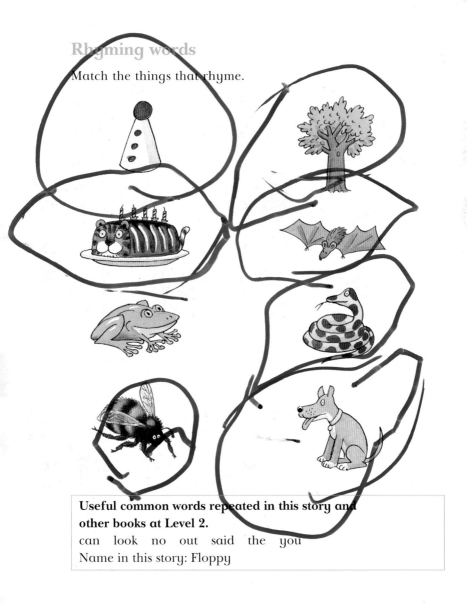

Useful common words repeated in this story and other books at Level 2.

can   look   no   out   said   the   you

Name in this story: Floppy